SIR GAWAIN
+ AND THE +
GREEN
KNIGHT

To Sebastian, Lada, Alan and Laurence ∽ M.M.

To my son Mark ∽ M.F.

First published 2004 by
Walker Books Ltd
87 Vauxhall Walk, London SE11 5HJ

10 9 8 7 6 5 4 3 2 1

Text © 2004 Michael Morpurgo   Illustrations © 2004 Michael Foreman

The right of Michael Morpurgo and Michael Foreman to be identified as author
and illustrator respectively of this work has been asserted by them in accordance
with the Copyright, Designs and Patents Act 1988

This book has been typeset in Golden Cockerel

Printed in China

British Library Cataloguing in Publication Data:
a catalogue record for this book is available from the British Library

ISBN 0-7445-8646-1

www.walkerbooks.co.uk

SIR GAWAIN
AND THE
GREEN
KNIGHT

AS TOLD BY
MICHAEL MORPURGO

ILLUSTRATED BY
MICHAEL FOREMAN

WALKER BOOKS
AND SUBSIDIARIES
LONDON · BOSTON · SYDNEY · AUCKLAND

THINK YOURSELF BACK IN YEARS, MY **FRIENDS**

– not as far as ancient Greece and the siege of Troy, nor as far as Romulus and Remus and Rome, but to Britain after the Romans had gone, a Britain in the early mystical mists of her most turbulent times, striving always to keep the invader at bay, and to make of herself a place where people could live out their lives in peace and safety and prosperity. Many kings came and went, many invaders and conquerors, and as the battles raged throughout the land there was great grief and suffering, and terrible hunger too.

Then, as the myth goes – and whether it is the myth of story or the myth of history is for you to decide – then there came a king who would lead the people of Britain out of the darkness of their misery and into the sunlight at last. His name was Arthur. Never had there been a braver, more noble king than this. Saved at birth, hidden away, then plucked from obscurity and chosen to be High King by the magical powers of Merlin, he drew the sword from the famous stone and not long afterwards gathered about him at Camelot all those great Knights, who had goodness at heart, who shunned all greed and pride, the finest and fiercest Knights in the kingdom, who fought only for right and for the wellbeing of others and of their kingdom. You know their names as well as I do from stories that have come down to us through the ages: Sir Lancelot, Sir Percivale, Sir Galahad, Sir Tristram –

dozens of them, too many to be listed here – and Sir Gawain, of course, who was the High King's nephew.

My story is of Gawain. Of all the tales of the Knights of the Round Table his is the most magical and the one I most love to tell. For Gawain, as you will shortly see, was as honest and true as a Knight of the Round Table should be, as kind and chivalrous and courteous, as brave as any other, and stronger in battle than any, except Lancelot. But Gawain was headstrong, too, and more than a little vain; and as this story will show, sometimes not as honest or true as he would want himself to have been: much like many of us, I think.

So, to his story, the story of Sir Gawain and the Green Knight.

IT WAS ✚ ✚ ✚ ✚ ✚ that time of the year when all King Arthur's Knights gathered to celebrate the birth of their Lord and Saviour, Jesus Christ. For fifteen joyous days, after holy Mass each morning there was nothing but feasting and dancing and singing, and hunting and jousting too. Jousting was the favourite sport, each of them striving to unseat the mighty Sir Lancelot – but rarely succeeding of course. And all was done in fun, in a spirit of great comradeship, for they were happy to be together once more, at this blessed time. During the year these lords were so often parted from one another, and from their ladies, as they rode out through the kingdom on their dangerous missions. So this was a time when love and friendship was renewed, a time to celebrate with their young king all their achievements and their great and good purpose: to bring peace to the land, and make of it a kingdom as near to a heaven on earth as had never before been achieved in Britain, nor in any other land, come to that.

On New Year's Eve, after evening Mass had been said in the chapel and generous new year's gifts exchanged, the High King and Guinevere, his queen, came at last into the great hall where all the lords and ladies were waiting to dine. No one could begin the feasting until they came, of course, so as you can imagine they cheered them

to the rafters when they saw them. Guinevere had never looked so gloriously beautiful as she did that evening, and there were gasps of admiration from around the hall, from lords and ladies alike.

With Arthur on one side of her and Gawain on the other, Guinevere sat down at the high table, which was set on a splendid dais draped all about with silk and richly hung with the finest tapestries from Toulouse and Turkestan. Then, with drummers drumming and pipers piping, the servants came in carrying the food on great silver plates, piling each table high with roasted meat, capons and venison and pork, and fish fresh-baked in sea salt, and baskets of crusty bread, and steaming soups. Truly there was enough to feed the five thousand, though there were only five hundred there to eat it. As they poured out

the wine and ale, filling every goblet to the brim, the scents of the feast that lay before them filled the succulent air, and their nostrils too, so that, their appetites whetted, they were all longing now to begin. But the High King and his queen sat there, not touching their food nor their drink either. Everyone knew that if they did not begin, then out of respect nor could anyone else. And everyone knew also why it was that the king was refusing to let the feast begin.

The great hall fell silent as Arthur rose to his feet. "You know the custom," he began. "I will not take one mouthful, nor one sip of wine, until I am told of some new and stirring tale, some wonderfully outlandish adventure, some extraordinary feat of arms so far unheard of. And it must be true, too. I don't want you to go making it up just so you can get at the food – some of you are good at the tall stories." They laughed at that, but as they looked around it became clear that none of them had a tale to tell. "What?" cried the High King. "What? Not one of you? Well then I see we must all go hungry. Such a pity. Isn't it strange how food you cannot eat always smells so wonderful? It needn't be a story, of course. It could be some new happening, some weird and wondrous event. If I can't have a story, then you'd better hope, as I do, that maybe some stranger will come striding in here right now and challenge us face to face. That would do. I'd be happy with that. Then we could all begin our feasting before the food gets cold." And with that he sat down.

At that very same moment, just as the High King had finished speaking, they heard a sudden roaring of wind, the rattle of doors and windows shaking and then, outside, the clatter of a horse's hooves on stone. The great doors burst open, and into the hall rode the most awesome stranger anyone there had ever set eyes on. For a start he was a giant of a man, taller by two heads than any knight there, but not lanky and long, not at all. No, shoulder to shoulder he was as broad as any three men stood side by side, and his legs were massive – like tree trunks, they were. And you could see the man's arms were about as thick and strong as his legs. But that wasn't all. This giant was green: green from head to toe. Yes, bright green, I tell you, as green as beech leaves in summer when the sun shines through. And when I say the man was green, I don't just mean his clothes. I mean him. His face. Green. His hands. Green. The hair that hung down to his shoulders. Green. Only his eyes, horror of horrors, glowed red, blood red and glaring from under his heavy eyebrows, which were as green as the rest of him. Everyone in that hall simply gaped at him, at his hugeness and his greenness, and at his grimness too, for the man had a thunderous scowl on his face that struck terror into every heart.

Grim he may have been, but the giant was gorgeous, too – if such an apparition can ever be said to be gorgeous. He wore a tunic of green velvet with buttons of gleaming gold. Stirrups and spurs were all of gold, both encrusted with the brightest emeralds of the deepest green. And his horse! His warhorse was a monster of a creature – he had to be, just to carry this giant. The horse was green too, green from nose to hoof, from mane to tail. He was pawing at the ground, tossing his head, foaming at his bit; at least the foam was white. He looked every bit as bad-tempered as his master. They suited each other, those two.

Yet fierce though he seemed, the knight in green wore no war helmet and no armour either. He held no shield before him, and carried no spear, not even a sword at his side. Instead, the hand clutching the reins held a sprig of holly – green, naturally – which might have been laughable had everyone not already noticed what he was carrying in his other hand. It was an axe, but it was no ordinary battle-axe. This weapon was a real head-cruncher. Yet the handle was most delicately carved – bright green of course, as was the cord that looped about it and the tassels that hung from it. Only the huge blade itself was not green. Curved like a crescent moon at the cutting edge, it was made of polished steel – a hideous widow-maker if ever there was one. Even the dogs, usually so fierce with any stranger, shrank back whining under the tables, their tails between their legs.

There came no cheery new year greeting from this green man, not even a ghost of a smile. In a thunderous, booming voice as terrifying as the man himself, he said, "So, who's in charge here?" No one answered him. "Well, come on. Speak up. Which of you is the king? It's him I've come to talk to, no one else." But as he rode around the hall, his blazing eyes scanning the lords and ladies on every side, no one spoke up. And you can understand why. Many of the knights sitting there in that hushed hall had come across all kinds of astounding and alarming looking creatures while out on their quests – dragons and monsters, goblins and ghouls – but never anything quite like this. Most sat there stunned to silence. Others kept quiet out of respect for their High King, wanting to hear how he would reply.

No one doubted for a moment that he would have the courage to speak up, and so he did. Indeed, as he rose to his feet he was smiling broadly. After all, hadn't he just been hoping for such a happening as this? "Welcome to Camelot, Sir Knight," he began. "I am the king you are looking for, I think. My name is Arthur. Believe me, you could not have arrived at a better moment. So please dismount and join our new year's feasting, and afterwards you can tell us perhaps why you have come here to our court."

The knight in green rode towards the dais and spoke directly to the High King, but more courteously now. "My thanks, great King. But I will not stay, nor keep you from your feasting. I will speak my purpose plainly. I cannot tell you how honoured I am to meet you at last, the great Arthur, High King of all Britain. I have heard, as all the world has heard, how you have made of this place the most wondrous kingdom on earth, and gathered around you the most worthy, courageous and chivalrous knights that ever lived. Looking about me I begin to wonder whether you deserve this glowing reputation at all. I mean no offence great King; as you can see from the sprig of holly I carry, I come in peace. If it were otherwise I'd be armed for a fight, would I not? But you see no armour on me, no helmet, no sword or spear, because it is not war I come for, but sport – well, a sport of sorts, anyway."

"If it's jousting you're looking for," the High King replied as politely as his irritation would allow, "or wrestling maybe, then daunting though you may look, Sir Knight, you'll find no lack of sport here, I assure you."

"But I joust and wrestle only with men," replied the Green Knight. "I see here nothing but beardless boys. It would be no contest. None of you would stand a chance against me. No, I have in mind something much more testing of a man's courage, and much more interesting for everyone. But I cannot imagine there will be anyone here brave enough to take me on."

"We'll see about that," the High King cried, his face flushing with sudden anger at the stranger's insulting tone. "Just get on with it for goodness' sake, and tell us what game it is you want to play. Our soup is getting cold."

The Green Knight laughed. "Why don't we just call it a New Year's

game?" he said. "I don't think any of you will ever have played it before, and nor have I. We'll soon see what stuff your Knights of the Round Table are made of, whether you're all you're cracked up to be." So saying, he held high his great axe. "Here is my battle-axe," he went on. "Is there anyone here in this hall brave enough to take it, I wonder? Whoever does will have one chance, and one chance only, to strike my head from my shoulders. I shall not resist or fight back. I shall not even flinch, I promise."

"Is that the game?" the High King asked, as incredulous as everyone else in the hall.

"Not quite," replied the Green Knight. "Here's how the game goes. If any knight has the courage to take up the challenge, then he will have to promise, on his honour, that in a year and a day from now he will submit himself to … let's call it a return match, shall we? Then it will be my turn to strike the same single blow, and it will be one of you who has to kneel there, bare his neck and take it – without resisting, without flinching. Well, who dares?"

If there was a hushed silence when he first came into the hall, the place was now still as death as he glared all around, waiting for someone to speak up. But even the bravest of the knights lowered their eyes. This was one challenge they all wanted to avoid if they could. The Green Knight wheeled his great warhorse and clattered about the hall looking down at them, a supercilious sneer on his lips. "I thought so. I thought so," he said, his mocking laughter ringing in the air.

"Where's your courage now? Where's that spotless honour, that perfect chivalry I've heard so much about? Is there no one here who has the stomach to take me on?" Still no one spoke. "Chickens, the lot of you. Worse than chickens, too. At least chickens cluck. I can see I'm in the wrong place. This can't be the court of King Arthur. It's a court of cowards."

Stung to fury now the High King had had enough. "Cease your insults!" he shouted. "None of us here is frightened of you. We're just speechless at the sheer stupidity of such a ridiculous duel. It's obvious that with an axe like that whoever strikes the first blow is bound to be the winner. But since you insist upon it, and are so brash and rude, I shall take up your challenge myself. So get down off that horse, hand me your axe and I'll give you what you asked for." And with that, King Arthur sprang down from the dais and strode across the hall towards the Green Knight, who dismounted and at once handed over his axe. "Make yourself ready, then," cried the High King, swinging the axe above his head, testing his grip, feeling the weight and balance of the weapon. The Green Knight looked on. He stood head and shoulders above the king, dwarfing him utterly. Unperturbed by the swishing axe, the Green Knight turned down the neck of his tunic and made himself ready.

At that moment Gawain stood up. "No!" he cried. And leaving the table he hurried across the hall to his uncle's aid. He bowed low before him. "Let me take your place, uncle. Give me this fight, please, I beg you. I shall teach this green and haughty man that in a fight there are no knights braver than your own. It is true that I am no braver than any other man here, I know that, but I am your nephew. Make this an uncle's gift to his nephew. Because the truth is, good uncle, that if I do lose my life I would not be much missed compared to you. You are our king, and this is too silly, too demeaning a venture for you. Lose you and we lose the kingdom. Lose me and there will always be others to come in my place."

"For goodness' sake make up your minds," said the Green Knight, shaking his head, "I do not have all day."

Ignoring the man's boorishness Gawain knelt before the king. "Let me prove myself worthy, uncle, worthy of being your Knight and your nephew too." There was much applause at this and many loud voices raised in support of Sir Gawain's plea. After thinking for a while the High King lifted his hand for silence, and taking Gawain's hand helped him to his feet. "As you wish, nephew," he said. "There's nothing I'd like better than to separate this man's great green head from his great green shoulders; but I willingly give the task to you. Strike boldly, nephew. If you do, I really cannot see, short of a miracle, how you will ever have to face him again in a year and a day. Here's the axe. You'll find it a bit heavy and cumbersome, but it'll do the job."

Gawain took the axe from him, gripped it firmly and turned now to face the Green Knight, who stood towering above him, his hands on his hips. To everyone there they looked like David and Goliath – and all were hoping and praying for the same unlikely outcome. "So," said the giant knight, "so we have a champion at last. Let's get on with it. But before we do I must know your name, and make sure we both understand and agree on the rules of the game."

"My name is Sir Gawain and I already know the rules of your foolish game," came the blunt reply.

"Good Sir Gawain, I'm glad it is you," said the Green Knight then, altogether more polite now than he had been so far. "I'll be honoured to take the first blow from a knight as noble and worthy as yourself, for you are known and revered throughout all Britain as a man of not only the greatest courage, but also the greatest integrity. Believe me, you will need both, and in full measure, for what I have in store for you. And just so there can be no misunderstanding, you must promise on your honour and in the hearing of everyone in this hall that a year and a day from now you will seek me out and find me, so that I can pay you back in kind for whatever you do to me today."

"I promise you willingly, on my honour as a Knight of the Round Table," Gawain replied. "But how shall I be able to find you? I don't even know your name, nor from what part of the country you come. Just tell me, and I'll be there, you have my word."

"Afterwards. I shall tell you all you need to know afterwards," said the Green Knight. "Once you have done your worst, I'll tell you exactly where to come and who I am." And with a smile that sent shivers even into brave Gawain's heart he went on, "I'll be looking forward to you calling on me in a year and a day. I'll be looking forward to it very much indeed."

With the smile still on his face, the Green Knight went down on one knee before Gawain, and bared his neck. "Do the best you can, Sir Gawain," he said. "Remember, you have only one chance."

"Make your peace with your maker," Gawain replied, running his finger along the blade.

Then, grasping the handle tight and putting his left foot forward, he took a deep breath and raised the great axe high above his head, the blade flashing blood red in the flames of the fire. Down it came and sliced right through the Green Knight's neck, cutting clean through bone and flesh and skin, severing the terrible head entirely and sending it rolling hideously across the floor towards the lords and ladies at their table. And the blood was not green, as you might have

imagined, but bright red like any man's, and it spurted freely from head and body alike.

But instead of toppling over, as everyone expected, that grotesque headless body rose up onto his feet and strode across the floor to where his head lay bleeding, the eyes closed in death. Snatching the baleful head up by the hair, he went straight to his horse, set one foot in the stirrup and swung himself up easily into his saddle as if nothing at all had happened. Suddenly those eyes opened and glared most horribly about the hall. Everyone was struck dumb with terror.

But worse was still to come, for then the mouth began to speak. "Well struck, Sir Gawain. Now I'm afraid you have your side of the bargain to keep, a promise you made freely and openly, in front of everyone here and in front of your king too. You must seek me out and find me at the Green Chapel, a year and a day from now. There I shall repay you, a blow for a blow, as we agreed. I am known everywhere as the Knight of the Green Chapel. Look into the sky as you go and follow where your eyes and your ears lead you. I shall be waiting. Be sure you come, Sir Gawain, or the world will know you for ever as a coward." He said nothing more, not one goodbye, but, turning his horse about, set spurs to his side and galloped from that hall, sparks flying from the horse's hooves as he went. Where he had come from no one knew; where he went to no one knew. But as you can well imagine, I think, all were glad to see him gone.

It was some time before anyone in the hall found voice to speak, and then it was the High King himself who at last broke the silence. He was as amazed and horrified as everyone else by what they had just witnessed, but he did not like to see his queen and his court so downhearted on this festive evening. "Come on now, let's not be upset," he said. "After all, this was just such a marvel as we were waiting for, was it not? And marvels like this are as much a part of new year at Camelot as carols and feasting. Like it or not, and I agree it wasn't a very appetizing spectacle, you have to admit we've never seen anything quite like it before, have we? And best of all it means we can now begin our feasting. So hang up your axe, Gawain, somewhere where we can all see it and be reminded of your courage, and come and join us. Let's eat, my friends. Let's drink. Let's be merry." And so they were – all but Gawain, whose thoughts, like ours must now do, ran on ahead of him to New Year's Day a year hence, to the dreaded day when he would meet that Green Knight once again at the Green Chapel.

BUT A WHOLE YEAR DOES NOT PASS IN THE TWINKLE OF AN EYE,

not for you, not for me, not for Gawain. Every season must take its time. After all the fun and feasting and frolicking of the new year is done, then comes unwelcome, fish-eating Lent, but even by now the first snowdrops have shown their pretty heads and the cold of winter has begun to lose its icy grip. A pale new sun drives away the last of winter's clouds. Primrose and daffodil bring promise of longer days, and grass and leaves grow green again. Blackbirds cackle in budding gardens and woodpeckers knock in hollow trees. The first cuckoo and the first lark tell us for sure it is spring again, and swallows and swifts bring us the hope of summer, skimming low over the hayfields, screeching around our chimney tops. Now we have mornings of soft valley mists and garden dews. Salmon rise in the rivers, and the gentle breeze of summer touches our cheeks. The earth itself warms with life, feeding the seeds that will soon grow and be feeding us. And all about us we hear now the humming of bees, the crying of lambs, the mewing of soaring buzzards. Soon enough, though, the harvest calls us to the fields and we must hurry, for we know from the chill in the evenings that autumn

is almost upon us. The trees dressed so brightly, so gloriously in brown and red and gold, stand and wait in dread for the rough winds of winter that will soon make stark skeletons of them again. Now we huddle inside once more before our fires, and through rattling windows watch the leaves fly and the green of the grass turn grey before our eyes.

AS EACH MONTH OF THE YEAR PASSED, 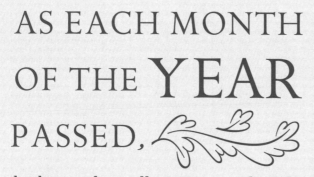 and the seasons came and went, it was hard for Gawain not to think from time to time of the terrible fate he must face – and sooner now, not later. Many a long night he lay awake, willing time to slow down: but time neither waits nor hurries on for any man. It was already Michaelmas moon, and he knew he must soon leave Camelot and be on his way. His spirits uplifted by the love of the king and queen, and by his brotherhood of Knights, Gawain stayed as long as he dared, until All Saints' Day. The last night before he was to leave they held a great feast in his honour, and everyone at Camelot, lords and ladies, squires and servants, did all they could to keep him merry. But try as they might the jokes and the laughter seemed flat and forced, the smiles thin, for all of them realized this was likely to be the last time they would dine with brave Gawain. No knight in that court was more well-loved and honoured than he. Bravely, but sadly, Gawain rose to his feet. "Uncle, good King, my dear friends," he said, "the time has come for me to say goodbye. You know where I have to go, what I have to do, and that God alone can save me and bring me home again. So pray for me. It's all you can do. Be sure that whatever happens, I will not dishonour you."

One by one each said their sad farewells: Sir Lancelot, Sir Galahad, Sir Bors, Sir Bedivere, every knight that was there, and Queen

Guinevere too, and all the ladies of the court, many of them weeping openly at this parting. Gawain put on it as brave a face as he could. "A man must do and dare," he said. "No more tears. I'll be back."

The next morning, after a sleepless night filled with fears and doubts, Gawain rose early and called for his servants to fetch him his clothes and armour. They put on first his doublet and fur-lined cape, which they fastened tight around his neck against the cold. They strapped on his armour, all brightly burnished, until he was covered in steel – thighs, arms, even his hands. Over it all they hung a heavy scarlet surcoat, wonderfully embroidered, and around this at his waist they tied a silken swordbelt of peacock blue. With his gold spurs at his heels and his sword in its sheath he was as ready as he would ever be to face any foe.

From his room Gawain went straight to the chapel to say Mass, and then at once to the courtyard to Gringolet, his waiting warhorse, who was as magnificently dressed and armoured as his master. Once he has settled in the saddle the servants handed him up his helmet. And what a helmet it was. Padded on the inside, it was polished and jewelled on the outside. The neckguard was strong enough to save him from even the most terrible of blows to the head. Once he had buckled on his helmet he was handed his shield, with his own coat of arms embossed upon it. This was a gold pentangle, a five-pointed star, each point representing a virtue to which any true knight must aspire: loving kindness, integrity, chivalry, loyalty and holiness. And etched on the back of the shield, where he could see it at a glance if ever his courage failed him, was the face of the blessed Virgin Mary herself.

Now as the snow fell about him he said his last farewell to his uncle and his king, who handed him his spear. "God go with you, nephew," said the High King.

"Godspeed!" the servants cried, every one of them sick at heart. Not one of them believed they would ever set eyes on him again.

Once across the drawbridge Gawain determined to put all his nagging fears and doubts behind him. He knew there was a long and dangerous journey ahead, and that he would need all his wits and courage just to survive. So he spurred Gringolet on and sang out loud to give himself courage, to give himself hope. But then as he wondered which way he should go, he heard again the Green Knight's voice in his head: "Look into the sky as you go and follow where your eyes and your ears lead you." Gawain looked up, and even as he looked, he heard above him the sound of singing, not of human voices but rather the singing of wings.

High above and ahead of him flew a flock of geese, pointing the way

north, a singing arrowhead in the sky. It was the sign Gawain knew he must follow, that would lead him sooner or later to the place he most dreaded on this earth ... the Green Chapel of the Green Knight.

In the deep of that bitter winter, Gawain rode on through the wastelands of Britain, always keeping the flying geese ahead of him and the wild mountains of Wales to his left. At night he lay often in the open, wrapped in his surcoat with no shelter at all, with only his horse beside to protect him from the icy winds. Food in that frosty land was scarce. All he had to live on were the nuts he could scavenge – those the squirrels and dormice had not already taken. Within a few days he found himself in the county of Wirral, where the people were as savage and inhospitable as Gawain had ever known. If he asked for food or shelter they drove him from their hovels with curses. And if ever he asked where he might find the Green Knight of the Green Chapel, they hurled insults and stones at him and would not answer.

Far from home now and far from friends Gawain rode, with only his guiding geese and Gringolet for company. Weakened by cold and hunger he often had to fight off wayside robbers who lay in wait for him, or wild animals that hunted him. In the dim of dusk one evening, as he rode through a forest, he was chased by a pack of ravenous wolves. With Gringolet too exhausted to gallop, Gawain dismounted, turned to face them and cut them down one by one as they came at him.

One time a fire-belching dragon blocked his path. Gawain at once speared him through the heart and went on his way. Wild and savage

men of the woods, boars and bulls and bears, this Knight saw them all off, even the three-eyed ogre of Orall who said he would not let him pass until Gawain had given him his horse to eat. "My Gringolet is for riding, not eating," Gawain declared, and drawing his sword attacked the ogre, who was twice his size. After a fierce battle that lasted all morning long Gawain at last dealt him a deathblow, and leaving the ogre lying there he mounted his horse again and rode on, following the geese ever northwards.

But it was not these dangers that troubled Gawain most. It was the cold. Sleeping or walking, the sleeting wind cut through the armour and chilled him to the very bone. The world had frozen white and hard around him, and as he went the knight was losing much of his strength and almost the last of his hope. He began to despair of ever finding the Green Chapel at all. There was no one to ask, no one to help him.

As he rode one day over those inhospitable hills, icicles hanging from the jagged rocks around him, Gawain looked up and saw that even his faithful geese had deserted him. "Now I will never find the place," he said to himself. "And by my reckoning it is Christmas Eve already." In his misery he prayed aloud to the Virgin Mary that in her mercy she would help him and by some miracle guide him to warmth and shelter that night, or he would surely die of the cold. Beneath him Gringolet plodded on gamely through the snow, though like his master he was weary now and stumbled more than once to his knees. He had had enough. So Gawain dismounted and they walked on together, their way taking them down into a ravine overhung on both sides by wizened trees, oak and hawthorn and hazel, the whole place so dark and dank that even the birds would not sing there.

Worse was to come. Once through the ravine they came to a swamp, where they sank so deep with every step that Gawain thought both he and Gringolet must sink altogether and never be found. Now he prayed again, even harder this time, his eyes tight shut, and crossed himself again, beseeching the Virgin Mary to save them. Then, on opening his eyes, he saw before him through the trees the towers of a wondrous castle. Out of the swamp they came, out of the shadows of the trees onto a wide sunlit plain, the great castle set in its midst.

"There's a welcome sight, Gringolet," he said. "Thanks be to God for it. We're saved. But I cannot walk one step further. Let me ride on

you just this short distance, and then, I promise you, you shall rest."
Gringolet stood for him, and so Gawain mounted, and rode across
the great plain towards the castle, which stood surrounded by a wide
moat and a palisade of pointed stakes. The castle glowed gold in the
evening sun – and what a castle it was! Massively built in stone, the
outer walls protected a great high hall, and around this splendid hall
there were so many towers and turrets and pinnacles that Gawain
could not count them, all of them more ornate and wonderful than
anything he had ever seen.

Patting Gringolet's neck, Gawain urged him on one last time. He
rode him right to the moat's edge, and was just about to call out when
the drawbridge came down and a smiling porter appeared at the
portcullis. "I wonder, good fellow," said Gawain, "whether you might
ask the lord of this fair house if I may stay awhile and rest."

"Of course, of course," cried the porter, "my master is not one to
turn away strangers. I'm sure you can stay as long as you need to."
With that, the portcullis was raised and at once Gawain found himself
surrounded by servants, squires and knights, all of them welcoming
him most warmly. Some took Gringolet away to a stable where that
poor tired horse was rubbed down and given all the hay and straw he
needed, whilst others led Gawain into the great hall of the castle,
where he saw a sight to warm his heart, and his body too – a huge,
crackling, roaring fire. Here, as the feeling came back to his hands and
feet, they took from him his helmet and his wet surcoat and armour

and gave him steaming mulled wine to drink, so hot that the cold was shivered out of him within minutes.

As he drank and warmed himself in front of the fire, into the hall strode the lord of that castle. The two knights greeted one another like old friends, though they had never set eyes upon each other before. "I thank you, good sir," said Gawain, "for all your kindness in welcoming me like this." Gawain felt the great strength of the man as they embraced, and saw it too in his build. Everything about him was big, his broad smile, his booming voice, his great wide shoulders and full round face, with a bushy beard to match, thick and beaver brown.

"Fine though your clothes are," said the lord, holding Gawain at arm's length, "we must have you at once out of your travelling clothes and into something – how shall I put it? – cleaner." And as they laughed together the lord called in his servants, who led Gawain away to a bedchamber finer than he had ever known.

The walls were hung all about with the finest of tapestries. The bed curtains and coverlets were of shining silk, intricately and exquisitely embroidered with birds and flowers. Servants brought dozens of sumptuous robes from which he could choose whichever one he thought suited him best. Then they led him back down to the great hall, where the lord and his court were all gathered to greet him. They sat him down by the fire, and at once a table was brought in and set for him. And then came the food he was longing for: thick seasoned soups, fish of every kind, baked in salt or grilled or stewed. He ate every bit and washed it down with more mulled wine.

All of this pampering had so lifted his spirits, so soothed his aching

bones, that Gawain soon felt completely renewed and restored. Being good hosts, the lord of the castle and his guests waited patiently until he had finished, and then at last the lord asked him what he and everyone had been longing to know. "Well, friend, will you tell us now who you are and from where you come?"

"I come from the court of the great King Arthur," he replied, "and my name is Sir Gawain." At this there were gasps of surprise and admiration, for Gawain's reputation for chivalry, courtesy and courage had gone before him. Every lord there aspired to be like him, and every lady there loved him on sight, for they could see that Gawain was as beautiful as he was brave.

By this time it was already close to midnight and the chapel bells were ringing, calling them to Christmas evensong. The lord of the castle led Gawain to his place of honour in the chapel and presented him to his wife, who sat opposite him across the aisle. She was a woman of such perfect beauty that Gawain found it difficult to concentrate on his prayers at all, though he knew he had much to thank his saviour for that day. She's even more beautiful than Guinevere, Gawain thought, closing his eyes not so much to pray as to keep himself from gazing at her in wonder. But it was impossible not to look at her. When he glanced up again he noticed at her side a much older lady, as warty and wrinkled as the ugliest toad that ever lived. A strange pair, Gawain thought: one a wretched old hag with an evil eye, a hairy chin and a warty nose, the other a paragon of

beauty with a face like an angel. But I must not let my mind think on her any further. You're in a chapel, Gawain, and she's another man's wife.

But after evensong was over Gawain could not help himself, and approached the lord's wife to talk with her. It was a brief meeting, long enough only for pretty compliments to be exchanged and to bid each other a fond goodnight. Then the lord led him to the fireside again and the two knights drank on together happily into the small hours, revelling in each other's company, for the two found much to love and admire in the other. "Will you stay on with us, Gawain?" said the lord, getting up to go to bed at last. "I know you'll make our Christmas feasting all the merrier. What do you say?"

"Gladly I will," Gawain replied. "Thank you." And embracing one another the two men parted and went upstairs to their beds. No knight ever slept more soundly than Gawain did that night.

So came Christmas morning, when they remembered with joy and thanks that holy child, born in a stable, who lived and died to bring peace and goodwill on earth. Carols there were in plenty that day, and solemn Masses sung in chapel, but chiefly it was a time for feasting and dancing. And whether dancing or feasting Gawain found himself often drawn to the beautiful lady of the castle, like a moth to a flame. At meals they were always seated side by side, while the lord seemed happy enough to have the hideous old hag for company. But dazzled though Gawain was by the ravishing beauty of his constant companion he managed to keep the talk between them polite and proper, as a good knight should. This was not at all easy, as she made it plainly obvious, to him and to everyone, that she had eyes only for him and was enthralled by every word he uttered. Thus distracted, Gawain hardly gave a thought to the fate that awaited him at the Green Chapel. But sometimes the dread of it did come over him like a dark cloud, and always the lady was there with her sparkling eyes and her infectious laughter, lifting him out of his despair, cheering his spirit.

For three long happy days, with precious little time for sleeping in-between, the festivities went on. No one, Gawain and the lovely lady least of all, wanted the last night of merriment to end, for they all knew that in the morning the celebrations would be over and Gawain, like many of the other guests, would have to leave. The midnight hour had long since come and gone, and Gawain was saying his goodbyes, when the lord of the castle took him by the elbow and led him aside so they could talk privately. "I don't want you to go, Gawain, my friend," he said. "Stay awhile, for my sake, a little longer."

"Sir," replied Gawain. "I wish I could. I would do anything in my power to repay you for the untold kindnesses you have shown me. Believe me, there is nothing in this world I'd like better than to stay here with you. But honour demands I should leave in the morning. I have no choice."

"Why?" asked the lord. "What is so urgent that it cannot be delayed just a few days? I know something has been troubling you, Gawain.

A man can tell, and a woman too. My wife has told me how even in the midst of great merriment your brow can suddenly darken as if you are afflicted by the most fearful thoughts and imaginings. Tell me what is troubling you, Gawain."

So Gawain told the lord his whole story, all that had happened the year before at King Arthur's court, and about the promise he had to keep with the Green Knight at the Green Chapel on New Year's Day. "So now you know, sir, why I must be on my way, why I don't wish to go, and why I must go. And I haven't left myself much time. I still don't know where I can find this Green Chapel."

At this the lord clapped him cheerily on the back. "Well, you don't have to worry about that," he said, "because the Green Chapel you talk of is only a few miles from here. I know the place well. When the time comes I'll have one of my servants take you there – it'll take half a morning, no more. So you see, you can stay on here and leave on the morning of New Year's Day itself. You'll be there in plenty of time."

"You're quite sure?" Gawain asked.

"Perfectly certain," replied the lord, putting an arm around him. "Listen, Gawain, for the next few days I want you to put aside all thoughts of that day and that place, and just enjoy yourself. Eat, drink and be merry; you know what they say – 'For tomorrow we die.'" And the lord's booming laughter rang around the hall.

Gawain, who was not able to laugh quite so wholeheartedly at this, did his best to put a brave face on it. "Then I shall stay," he said, "and gladly too. But how can I repay you for all this lavish hospitality, all this loving kindness? If there is ever any favour I can do for you, sir, you have only to ask and it shall be done."

"If there is, my friend, I shall ask," replied the lord. "You can be sure of it."

So Gawain stayed and they spent all the next day with the ladies, walking and talking, with more feasting and dancing that evening – always watched, Gawain noticed, by the ancient crone who followed them everywhere like a shadow, her eyes always fixed on Gawain as if she were examining his very soul. But even so the day was the most enjoyable yet, for there were now fewer guests there and at times Gawain had the lord and his delectable lady almost to himself.

After everyone else had gone to bed the two knights sat alone together, talking and musing late into the night, warming their feet in front of the fire. Then suddenly the lord of the castle leaned forward. "Tell me, Gawain, did you really mean it when you told me last night you would do me any favour I asked, or was it just talk?"

"Of course I meant it," Gawain replied. "Ask away, whatever you like."

"Well then," said the lord, a smile on his lips, "here's what I propose. I shall be going hunting every day for the next three days. After your long journey in the saddle the last thing you'll want is three days' hard hunting. So instead why don't you stay here and look after my wife and keep her company. She hates being left alone. Would you do that

for me? She'll look after you very well, I'm sure of that. She'll see your every wish fulfilled."

"I can't think of anything I'd like better," Gawain replied, and he meant it.

"But just one thing more," the lord went on. "I like games – I always have. I should like the two of us to a play a little game. These are the rules: whatever I bring back from my day's hunting, whatever I catch, I will give to you. And in return, whatever comes your way back here, however small or insignificant it may seem, you will return it to me at the end of the day. Does that sound fair? Shall we play?"

"Why not?" said Gawain, and laughing, they shook hands on it. "Here's hoping, for my sake, you have a good day's hunting."

"You too," replied the lord of the castle. "Let's seal our pact with more wine, shall we?" And so indeed they did, with more and more wine, until at last the fire died at their feet, and the cold of night crept into the hall and forced them up to bed.

❧❧ EARLY THE NEXT MORNING AS GAWAIN SLEPT ON,

deep in his dreams, the lord was up and dressing for the hunt, as was every other man in the castle, servant, squire and knight. Mass was said, as always. Straight away afterwards they went to have their morning broth as the horses were readied in the snowy courtyard outside, the deerhounds gambolling at their feet, their tails waving, wild with excitement. Then, with the lord and his followers mounted, the whole company clattered out over the drawbridge, their hot breaths – horse, man and hound alike – mingling in the frosty air.

Once across the plain and into the woods the horns sounded, sending the willing hounds to their work. They soon set up such a yelping and barking and baying that the whole valley resounded, sending shivers of fear into the hearts of every deer in the forest. Even as the deer heard it they knew that there was no hiding place now, that speed was their only saviour, that the slowest amongst them would surely die that day. So they ran for their lives, stags and hinds, bucks and does, flitting through the sunlit glades, leaping the roaring streams, clambering up rocky ravines, trying all the while to outrun the hounds, to shake off the hunters. But the deerhounds had seen them now and were hard on their heels. Waiting ahead of the deer, hidden in the forest, were the beaters, who, setting up a sudden

terrible hullabaloo, turned them and drove them back towards the hunters' arrows, towards the tearing teeth of the hounds. Time after time the archers let loose their arrows and another deer would fall. Time after time the hounds cornered an old stag and dragged him down. Hot with the chase but never tiring, the lord and his hunters rode on all day, following the deer wherever they fled, down deep wooded valleys, up over rocky moors. Many a deer died that morning, but many also were allowed to escape. The lord, as considerate a huntsman as he was a kind host, saw to it that they killed only the old and the weak, and allowed the others to live on.

All the while, back in the castle Gawain slumbered on. Hovering on the edge of a dream he was not sure at first if the footstep he heard was real or imagined. Waking now, he sat up and pulled back his bed curtain, just a finger's breadth. The lady of the castle, that beautiful creature, was there in his room, in her nightgown. She was closing the door silently behind her. Quickly Gawain lay back again and pretended to be fast asleep. His heart beating fast, he heard the soft footsteps, heard the bed curtains being drawn back, felt the bed sag as she sat down beside him.

Now what do I do? thought Gawain. She cannot have come here simply to talk about the weather, can she? Perhaps I had better find out what she wants. So, pretending he was just waking up, he turned on his back and stretched and yawned. Then he opened his eyes. He did his best to feign surprise, but he knew himself it wasn't a very convincing performance.

"Awake at last, Sir Gawain! I never took you for a sleepyhead," she began, her eyes smiling down at him. "So at long last I have you at my mercy."

"If you say so, my lady," Gawain replied, sitting up and trying to gather his wits about him as he was speaking. "You know I would do anything in my power to please you, lady," he went on, struggling to find the right words. "But I think I should much prefer to get up and get dressed first – if you don't mind, that is."

"But I do mind," she said reproachfully, and she shifted a little nearer to him on the bed. "I mind greatly. I have the great Sir Gawain close beside me. Do you think I would let him go? Would any lady let him go? I don't think so. I know you are renowned throughout the land for your courtesy, your chivalry and your honour. But my husband is off hunting with his friends, and after last night's merrymaking everyone else is still asleep. We are all alone." She leant over him, her lovely face, her soft skin close to his.

"Lady," he replied, "I'll be honest with you. God knows I'm not nearly as honourable as I'd like to be, nor as I'm made out to be. I wouldn't ever want to upset you, dear lady, but why don't we just talk? I like talking. I'm good at talking. I can be funny, serious, charming or thoughtful – whatever you like."

The lady laughed, took Gawain's hand and drew him closer again. "Dear Gawain," she said, looking deep into his eyes so that his heart all but melted, "there isn't a lady in this land who wouldn't die to be where I am now. In you I have everything a woman could desire – beauty, strength, charm. You are as truly courteous and chivalrous a knight as I have ever known." She sighed longingly and caressed him so tenderly with her eyes that Gawain almost gave in.

"I am very flattered, lady, that you should think so highly of me. I will try therefore to live up to these high ideals of knighthood you say I possess, and to which certainly I aspire. I will be your servant and your true knight, not wanting ever to hurt you or harm you in any way, nor ever to take advantage. I want only to protect you."

At this the lovely lady threw up her hands in despair. "Gawain, you disappoint me," she said. "But I'm not leaving this room without a kiss. As my knight you owe me that at least. Deny me that, and you would

hurt me deeply." One kiss, thought Gawain, where's the harm in that? As long as I don't enjoy it too much, it will be fine.

"As your knight I would never want to hurt you, lady," Gawain replied. "As your servant I will obey, willingly. Kiss away, my lady." And so she kissed him long and lovingly, and then quickly left the room.

Stunned by the kiss, Gawain sat there confused, relieved she was gone and yet longing for a second kiss. He washed and dressed swiftly and went downstairs, where all the ladies were waiting for him. As well as the lady of the castle he had a dozen other ladies looking after him that day. They tended to his every need, so, as you can well imagine, Gawain had a fine time of it. But wherever he went, whatever he did, he felt that ancient crone, that wrinkled hag, always watching him – and usually from somewhere behind him, so that by the end of the day Gawain had a dreadful crick in his neck.

As the sun set through the windows of the great hall they heard the drawbridge go rattling down. Rushing to look they saw the hunters spurring into the darkening courtyard, their horses' hooves sparking as they struck the cobbles. Great was the excitement when into the hall strode the lord of the castle, mud-spattered from the hunt, a huge deer slung over his shoulder. This he laid down at once at Gawain's feet. "Here you are, Gawain, my friend," he cried triumphantly. "Look what I have for you. I have twenty more like this, and all of them are yours, as I promised. Well? How do you think I have done?"

"Wonderfully well, my lord," Gawain began, choosing his words carefully. "But I am afraid you're going to be very disappointed in me, because all I have to offer you in return is this." And with that Gawain stepped forward, put his arms around the lord of the castle and kissed him once on the cheek, very noisily so that everyone should hear it.

Laughingly the lord wiped his cheek with the back of his hand. "Well, it's better than nothing, I suppose," he said, "But I'd have enjoyed it all the more if I'd known how you came by such a kiss."

"That you will never know," Gawain replied. "It wasn't part of our agreement. I did not ask you how you killed your deer, did I? No more questions, my lord. You have had all that was owing to you, and that's that."

"Fair enough, my friend," said the lord of the castle. "I'm starving. I shall bath first, then we shall eat and drink and be merry again."

Long into the night the two of them ate and drank, and talked together and laughed. Then, over the last goblet of wine – and sensibly they had left the finest wine till last – the two knights made again exactly the same pact between them for the following day. "And I'd like something a bit more interesting this time if you can manage it," laughed the lord of the castle, as they went upstairs to their rooms.

"I'll do my best," said Gawain. "I promise."

By the time the cock had crowed three times the lord was out of his bed and dressing. As before, Mass was said, and a quick breakfast

65

taken. Then the lord and his huntsmen were out in the cold grey of the dawn, mounting up and eager to be gone once again. The hounds too were keen to be off, their noses already scenting the air. Upstairs in his bedchamber as the hunt rode away Gawain heard none of this. He was dead to the world, sleeping off the heady excesses of the night before.

Far over the hills the hunting party went into a deep valley of thorns and thickets where they knew the wild boar roamed. It wasn't long before the hounds picked up a scent and gave voice, their howls echoing as loud as the huntsman's horn so that the whole valley rang with the terrible din of it. Baying in chorus the bloodhounds splashed on through a murky bog towards an overhanging cliff face, at the foot of which lay great piles of tumbled rocks and rugged crags. Here they stopped and bayed so dreadfully that the huntsmen knew the beast must be hidden in there somewhere, deep in some cave or cleft; but neither man nor hound dared go in after him.

Then one of those dark rocks seemed suddenly to heave itself to life and become a raging boar. Out of nowhere he came, charging straight at them, the biggest boar the lord had ever seen, and the meanest too. At a glance they could see he was old – he had to be, with tusks as huge as his. If he was old then he must be wily too, and this one was still nimble on his feet. Truly a formidable foe, this bristling monster, enraged at his tormentors, tossed his tusks furiously at the bloodhounds as he came towards them, and threw them aside as easily as if they had been helpless pups. And believe me, those he caught on the points of his tusks never rose again, but afterwards lay there dead and bleeding on the ground, a piteous sight. Bravely the hounds leapt at him and bravely he defended himself, spearing through the first one, then another, so that soon the pack bayed for blood no more but moaned and whined in its fear and grief, and hung back, unwilling to attack this monster again. In desperation the huntsmen tried shooting at him with their bows, but the arrows simply bounced off his bristling hide. They hurled their spears at him, but every one of them splintered on impact.

Now hunters and hounds both stood back, gazing in awe at this invincible beast as he escaped from them yet again, and wondering if at last they had met their match. But without a thought for his own safety the lord went after him, charging through the thickets and hallooing so fiercely, that, seeing his courage and determination, the huntsmen and the bloodhounds followed. This hunt was not over yet.

Back at the castle Gawain lay awake, but sleep was still in his head. What happened next he half expected. He heard the door open and the lady steal softly towards his bed. This time at least he was ready for her. As she parted the bed curtain, he sat up. "Good morning, my lady," he said cheerily.

She sat down beside him and stroked his brow softly. "What? Just good morning?" she wheedled. "Is that all I'm worthy of? Did I teach you nothing yesterday? Did we not kiss then, and now it is just 'good morning'?"

"Lady," Gawain replied, "It is not for me to offer to kiss you. If I tried to kiss you and you did not want it, then I'd be in the wrong, would I not?"

"How could I ever not want it?" she said, playing him with her shining eyes. "And even if I didn't want it, I could hardly stop you from kissing me, could I?"

"I would never do that," Gawain protested. "Where I come from no knight ever threatens a lady with force. But if you really want to kiss me, then please don't let me stop you. After all, a kiss from a lady to her knight is quite acceptable." So the lovely lady leant towards him and kissed him so sweetly that Gawain almost swooned with the joy of it. He wanted it never to stop. But stop it must, before it was too late. Breathless, Gawain pulled back and held her at arm's length. "Look," he said, "why don't we just talk? It's less dangerous."

"Oh, Gawain," complained the lovely lady. "Sometimes I'm not sure

I believe you are Sir Gawain at all. You are supposed to be the most chivalrous knight in the entire world. Isn't the sport of love among the most important of all the arts of chivalry? Doesn't a true knight fight for his love? Or have I got it wrong? Yet you sit there and say no words of love to me. Just to get a kiss out of you is like getting blood out of a stone. Is it that you don't like me? Am I not attractive to you, is that it?"

"Of course I do. Of course you are," Gawain replied.

"Then what are you waiting for?" she said, exasperated. "Here I am. My lord has gone hunting. We are alone. Teach me all you know of love, Gawain."

Now Gawain had to reply with all the skill and tact he could command, for he had to put her off without displeasing her, and that was not going to be easy. "Fair lady," he began, "just to have you near me, and to look at you, is enough. But as for the sport of love, I think you're much more skilled in that than I am. In that regard I'm just a clumsy knight, but I am a knight all the same, who must live in honour or die in shame. Having my honour always in mind I will do all I can to please you."

Still she stayed and tried to tempt him more, and again he resisted – but it was hard. In time, though, it became a game between them, a sport they both enjoyed, and at the end of it neither was the winner. But there was no loser either, so they could both be happy. They parted in friendship and love – and with a kiss so long and languorous that for several minutes after the lady had left, Gawain's head was still spinning.

He took his time getting up, for there was no hurry. Afterwards he went straight to Mass and prayed for God to give him strength to resist the lady, but also strength to face up to the trial he knew he must soon endure in the Green Chapel. All day long this fateful confrontation was in the back of his mind, but fortunately there were plenty of pleasant distractions to occupy him – particularly the ladies of the castle, who again did all they could to entertain him. Even that wizened old crone gave him a smile. Not a pretty smile, it's true, but a smile all the same.

While Gawain luxuriated in all these creature comforts and delights, the lord of the castle was still out chasing his fearsome boar. Over hills and dales the hounds and huntsmen chased that beast. Yet strong though the boar was, he tired at last, and knew his legs could carry him no further. On the banks of the rushing stream he made his last stand. Setting his back in a cleft in the rocks he dared them to come on. Foaming at his mouth and snorting his defiance, he faced them, pawing the earth in his fury and tearing at the ground with his terrible tusks. On the other side of the stream the huntsmen hesitated. They whooped and hallooed at the bloodhounds to keep them at their task, but like their masters none had the strength or courage to close and make the kill.

Only the lord himself dared try to finish it. Dismounting from his horse he drew his great sword, and striding through the stream he ran at the beast, who had only one thought in his mind: to hook his tusks into this man's body and kill him before he was killed himself. Out he charged, head and tusks lowered. Sheer speed and power took the lord by surprise. Hitting him with all his force full in the chest, the beast caught him off balance and sent him sprawling, so that the two of them tumbled backwards together into the stream. Luckily for the lord the tusks had not dug too deep into his flesh, but only gashed him slantingly. Luckily too for him, but not for the boar, the beast had charged onto the point of his sword, which passed clean through his heart, killing him at once.

As the boar was swept away downstream, his teeth still bared with the fury of his last charge, the huntsmen came to their lord's aid. Dazed and bleeding, he was nearly drowning when they dragged him out. It took a while for them to retrieve the boar, for the stream was fast and had carried him far, and being even heavier now in death it took a dozen strong men to haul him up onto the bank. Lord and huntsmen gazed down at their quarry and shook their heads in wonder, for this was truly a giant among boars. Dead though he was, the whining bloodhounds would not go near him even now, still fearful perhaps that the beast might rise phantom-like to his feet and come after them once again.

Back at the castle, dallying contentedly on cushions before the fire, Gawain and the ladies of the castle heard at last the sound of the hunt returning, the hunting horns resounding in triumph as the huntsmen rode laughing into the courtyard. They knew the hunt had been successful, but none could have imagined what they were about to see. When the lord, blood-spattered and mud-spattered, came striding into the hall, that was alarming enough. Then they saw the servants behind him come staggering in, carrying between them, dangling from a pole, the most gruesome sight they had ever seen – a bristling monster of a boar. He looked so evil and ferocious even in death that many ladies there had to look away, fearing this ghastly creature might be some incarnation of the devil himself.

"Here you are, Gawain my friend," said the lord, beaming proudly. "He's yours, my gift to you, as I promised you. Is he big enough for you? Have we done well?" Gawain walked all around the great beast, marvelling at it.

"What a splendid creature!" he breathed. "And what a huntsman you must be. But there's blood on you, my lord. Are you hurt?"

"Just a scratch," said the lord of the castle. "I was lucky. It could have been a lot worse." And smiling, he went on, "And how about you, Gawain? Were you lucky today? What have you got to give me in return for this magnificent beast?"

"Not a lot," Gawain replied. "Just this." And, laughing, he stepped forward and kissed the lord twice, once on each cheek. "That's it, I promise you," Gawain shrugged. "And to be honest, my lord, I'm glad it wasn't more, because much as I like you, I really don't like kissing men with great bristly beards!" At that the two friends laughed out loud, as did everyone else in that great hall, except for the unfortunate boar of course.

All evening the laughter went on: as the boar's head was brought in at dinner, an apple in his gaping mouth; as they drank and danced and sang the night away. But fun though it was, Gawain could not enjoy himself fully, for with the lady of the castle constantly at his side and making eyes at him he had always to be on his guard. She doted on him so openly, so obviously, that Gawain thought it must surely soon offend the lord of the castle. But much to Gawain's relief the lord seemed not to notice at all what was going on. He was wrapped all the while in conversation with the hideous old hag, who even as she was talking to him still eyed Gawain, smiling toothily at him as if she knew something that Gawain didn't. Gawain found them both, hideous hag and lovely lady, unnerving and deeply unsettling.

Although Gawain managed politely to keep that lovely lady at bay all evening, he could feel those pleading eyes slowly weakening his will to resist. He made up his mind to leave the castle the next morning and be on his way before he did something he would regret. He stood up. "Dear friends," he said, "I do not want to break the spirit of this feast, but I have stayed long enough and really think I should be off tomorrow morning."

"Nonsense!" cried the lord. "You shall do no such thing. I've told you, my friend, the Green Chapel you seek is only a few miles away. You can stay all day tomorrow, leave the following morning and easily be on time for your meeting at the Green Chapel. I shall be very hurt if you leave us before you need to. So will my wife and everyone here, too."

There was such a clamouring for him to stay that Gawain knew he could not refuse them. "I don't want to hurt anyone's feelings – and certainly not yours, my lord," Gawain said, "not after all you have done for me. So I shall stay as you command me."

"A wonderfully wise decision, Gawain," said the lord, "and all the better because it will give us another chance to play our game one last time, won't it? I'm off hunting first thing tomorrow as usual, so you can stay here and enjoy yourself as you will. When I get back in the evening we shall see what I have for you and you have for me. And

Gawain my friend, all I've had from you so far in this game is kisses. How about something different for a change?"

"I'll do my best," replied Gawain. But although he was laughing with everyone else, he was not at all happy to be playing the game again. He knew the risks that came with it.

"And now to bed," said the lord, yawning hugely. "I shall sleep like a log tonight."

So off they all went to bed, the servants lighting their way upstairs. The lord did sleep soundly, but for most of the night Gawain hardly closed his eyes at all. He lay there troubled mightily by all the trials and temptations he knew the next day would bring, and fell into a heavy sleep at last just as dawn was breaking. He heard nothing of the hunt gathering in the courtyard below his window, nothing of the yelping of impatient foxhounds, nor the snorting and stamping of horses eager to be gone. Gawain slept through it all.

The lord of the castle, refreshed from his night's sleep, rode hard across the fields, his huntsmen and hounds behind him. And what a beautiful morning it was too, with the clouds above them and the ground beneath them rose pink with the rising sun. But the fox cared little about that, for he had already heard the dreadful baying of foxhounds hot on the scent, and wanted only to put as much distance between them and himself as he could. The fox was fast, too, faster than any hound and he knew it, but he also knew they were stronger than him, that hounds did not tire as he would. Speed might help him, but only his cunning could save him. So he darted this way and that to bewilder them, weaving and doubling back on himself in amongst the rocks, fording as many streams as he could find, all to outwit the hounds and put them off the scent. Time and again he thought he had escaped them, but the hounds were not so easily fooled, and with so many noses to the ground they soon picked up his scent again and gave voice to tell him so.

As he slowed, they came on still faster, all in a pack, the huntsmen sounding their horns and hallooing loud so that the valleys rang with the song of the hunt, a song no wild creature ever wants to hear, the poor fox least of all. On he ran, his heart bursting, desperate to escape, to find some bolthole to hide where the hounds would not find him. But he was out on the open plain now, where there was nowhere to hide. All he could do was run. Catch me they may, thought the fox, but at least I'll lead them a merry dance before they do.

Gawain slept late that morning. He was deep in dreams when he felt a sudden shaft of brightness falling across his face. The lady of the castle came out of the sunlight, out of his dreams, it seemed, towards the bed, smiling as she came. "What? Still asleep, sleepyhead?" she laughed gaily. "It's a lovely morning out there. But, to be honest, I'd far rather be in here with you."

Still trying to work out whether he was dreaming or not, Gawain

saw that she was not wearing the same nightgown as before, but a robe of finest shimmering silk, white as cherry blossom and trimmed with ermine. She wore dazzling jewels in her hair and around her neck. She had never looked more beautiful. This time there was no preliminary banter whatsoever. She came straight to him as he lay there and kissed him at once on the lips. Now Gawain knew he really was awake. Her kiss was so inviting, so tantalizingly tender. "Oh Gawain," she breathed, "forget you are a knight just this once. Forget your chivalry and your honour."

It was lucky for Gawain that she had reminded him at that moment of his knightly virtues. "Dear lady," he said, desperately trying to rein himself in. "You have a gentle lord as a husband, who has shown me nothing but the greatest hospitality and friendship. I would not and I will not ever cheat him nor dishonour him. We can talk of love all you want, lady, but that is all."

"It is not talk I want," the lovely lady protested. "Let this opportunity pass, Gawain, and you will regret it for ever. Or is it perhaps that there is someone you already love more than me, someone you are promised to? Tell me the truth, Gawain."

"No, fair lady, I am promised to no one. And the truth is that although I have never in my life known anyone fairer than you, I do not want to promise myself to anyone just yet, not even you."

At this she moved away from him, shaking her head sadly. "How I wish you had not said that, dear Gawain," she sighed. "That's the trouble with truth – it cuts so deeply. But I asked for it, so I mustn't complain. I see now that I cannot hope to alter your mind or your heart. But couldn't you, in knightly courtesy and still protecting your honour, couldn't you at least give me one last kiss? As friends?"

"Why not?" replied Gawain. "After all, a kiss is just a kiss." And she leant over him and kissed him so gently, so softly, so sweetly, that Gawain very nearly forgot himself again.

"One last thing," she said, getting off the bed. "Will you let me have something of yours to take away with me, to remember you by, a token of some kind, a glove perhaps?"

"But I have brought nothing worthy enough to give you, dear lady," Gawain replied. "I wish I had, but I cannot give you just a dirty old glove. A lady like you deserves only the best, and I would far rather give you nothing at all than something unsuitable or insulting. Why don't we instead simply treasure the memories we have of one another? I shall not forget you, fair lady, I promise you that."

"Nor I you," replied the lady. "But all the same, it would please me so much if you would accept this memento of our time together." And taking a ruby ring off her finger, she offered it to him.

"I cannot take this, sweet lady," said Gawain, although he was touched to the heart by the generosity of this gesture. "If I can't give you a gift, then I must not accept one, and certainly not one as precious and valuable as this." She tried again and again to persuade him to take it, but he refused her every time, politely but firmly.

She wasn't finished yet, though. "All right then," she said at last, "if you won't take this, then will you instead accept something more simple, perhaps, something that has no real value at all but will remind you of me whenever you see it? Please, Gawain, it is only a little thing." With that she took from around her hips a wonderful belt of green silk richly embroidered in gold. "Take this, dear Gawain," she pleaded. "It's not much, but I have always worn it close to me. So if you were to do the same I should in some way always be close to you. Do it for my sake, to please me."

"Dear lady," Gawain replied, "I do not want to upset you, believe me, nor for us to part on bad terms. You call this a little thing, but yet it is a pretty thing, and I can see that it has been exquisitely crafted. It is still far too generous a gift, when I have none for you in return."

"This is more than a pretty thing, you know," the lady replied. "It was woven by an enchantress, so that whoever wears this belt can never be killed, not by a witch's cunning spells, nor by a dragon's raging fire, nor by the strongest and most deadly knight in all the land. Wear this belt around you, Gawain, and you are truly safe from all dangers."

"All dangers?" Gawain asked her, pondering hard on everything she had just told him.

"All dangers, I promise you," said the lovely lady, dangling the belt before his eyes.

This is too good a chance to turn down, thought Gawain. If what she says is true, then I could wear this belt tomorrow when I meet the

Green Knight, and no matter what happens I need not die. This belt would protect me. The offer was just too timely, too tempting. So at last he accepted the gift, taking it from her and thanking her from the bottom of his heart. "I will wear it always, and whenever I put it on, I promise I will think of you."

"Then I have won a little victory at last," laughed the lady, clapping her hands in joy. "I am so happy. But I have one very last favour to ask you, Gawain. You won't ever tell my lord and husband about this gift, will you? It might make him very jealous. It must be our secret, and our secret alone. Do you promise?"

"I promise, fair lady," Gawain replied. Although he did not feel at all comfortable about any of this, neither the gift nor the promise he had made, yet he did feel a lot easier in his mind about his encounter with the Green Knight the next morning.

The lady of the castle gave him one last kiss, and left him clutching the belt tightly and relishing again the three sweet kisses she had given him that morning. It was mid-morning by now, so hiding away the silken belt under his mattress, where he could find it later, Gawain dressed quickly. Then straight away he went down to Mass, and afterwards confessed all his sins – of which, as we know, there were more than usual that morning. So, freed of all cares now by both priest and belt, lucky Gawain was able to pass the rest of his day mingling with the ladies of the castle, who kept him more than happily occupied. He was so absorbed by the charm of their company that he scarcely gave a thought to what lay ahead of him the next day.

Out on the plain the poor old fox was not having such a happy time. He knew in his heart that his running days were over, but as every living creature will do in the struggle to survive, he tried his utmost to cling onto life as long as he could. Often he went to ground and lay there in the earthy darkness, his frantic heart pounding, hoping each time that the hounds would pass him by. But foxhounds carry their brains in their noses. No fox's scent ever escapes them. Once discovered, the fox lay low in his den for a while as the hounds gathered outside, baying for his blood, scrabbling at the earth to dig him out.

There are always
many ways out of a fox's den. Maybe he
would find some unguarded exit, and then make a run for it, bolting
off as fast as his legs could carry him. But, weakened as he now was,
he was not fast enough and the hounds were running more strongly
than ever as they closed in for the kill.

Poor Reynard. He made it to one last earth, and as he lay there he
knew he could run no more. He had two choices: to wait there in
terror only to be dug out and torn to pieces, or to end it now and get
it over with. His choice made, the brave old fox darted up the tunnel
into the light and there the lord of the castle was waiting, his sword
at the ready to spear him through. So mercifully the fox found the
speedy death he had sought. The huntsmen cheered wildly as the lord
held the fox up high by his tail, while the hounds howled at the lord
to be given their prey. But the lord bellowed loud above their baleful
baying. "Not for you, my friends," he cried. "This one I shall keep for
Gawain." So instead of the meat and skin and bone they craved he
gave them laughingly a pat on the head, then mounted his horse again
and rode home across the wide plain, the setting sun making long
shadowy giants of men and horses and hounds alike.

Back in the castle the lord strode at once into the great hall, the fox limp in his arms. Straight up to Gawain he went. "He may not look like much to you," he said, "but I can tell you this cunning old fox led us a merry old dance all day long. So he's all I've got to show for a whole day's hunting, and he's yours of course, as I promised. I'm just hoping you did a lot better today. What is it you have for me? Something special I hope. All I've had so far is kisses."

"I'm sorry to say, my lord," Gawain replied, laughing, "that kisses are all you'll get today as well, because they're all I got: but there is at least some good news for you, for today I'm going to give you not one, not two, but three!" And saying this he put his arms around the lord of the castle and kissed him affectionately and noisily three times, each time trying to avoid his bristling beard.

"I mean no offence, Gawain," said the lord, "but I have to say that I think you've had rather the better of our little game. But then I shouldn't grumble, for we both played by the rules, did we not?"

"We did," Gawain replied, but as he spoke he found it hard to look his friend in the eye.

That last evening they laid on a magnificent feast for Gawain. The whole castle resounded with carolling and dancing, and as they sat at the table joyous laughter rang through the rafters. Succulent venison they ate, and crackling pork, and all manner of spicy soups that warmed Gawain to the roots of his hair and set his scalp tingling. All evening long, every heart was alive with joy. No one ever once scowled or frowned, not even the usually surly old hag who seemed always to skulk about the castle. She drank her fill like everyone else, and smiled often at Gawain. But Gawain still found her a very troubling presence because when she smiled at him her eyes seemed to look right through him and see into his soul, where all his darkest secrets lay.

By now Gawain knew that he had had more than enough to drink, and that he must say his farewells whilst he still had his wits about him. He stood up, and lifted his goblet in a toast to all his new-found friends around the table. "May God bless you all for your many kindnesses to me these last few days," he said. "I have spent the most wonderful week of my life with you, basking in the warmth of your company, and I shall never forget it. I'd stay with you if I could, sir, you know I would. I don't want to go at all, but I must. I am a Knight of the Round Table, and tomorrow I have a promise I must keep. So if you will, lend me the guide you offered me, and let him show me the way to the Green Chapel, where I must face whatever God decides my fate should be."

The lord now also rose to his feet, and put his arm around Gawain's shoulder. "Like you, Gawain, I always keep my promises," he said. "You shall have your guide. He will be ready for you at dawn tomorrow, it is all arranged. He won't get you lost. Don't you worry, we'll get you where you have to go."

Then each lady in turn said her sorrowful goodbye to Gawain,

kissing him fondly – even that ancient crone had her turn. Then came the lady of the castle, who kissed him most tenderly, looking lovingly into his eyes one last time. The knights too came to embrace him, all of them wishing him good luck and Godspeed, until at last only the lord of the castle was left. "God keep you safe tomorrow, Gawain," he said, "and until we meet again."

Gawain was lost for words as they embraced one another lovingly and parted. Then he stood alone in the empty hall before the dying fire, and could think of nothing now but his meeting with the Green Knight the next day. He drank more wine, but even wine could not put it out of his mind. Maybe the silken belt is not enchanted at all, he thought. And even if it is, will it be strong enough to save my neck? Have I the courage to go through with this? Must I do it? Once in his bed these questions would not leave him, would not allow him the blessed oblivion of the sleep he longed for. All that long night he lay awake, hoping and praying most fervently that the green silken belt would save his neck – for he knew nothing else could.

The first crow of the cockerel sent a shiver of fear through him, but he clenched his jaws and his fists, gathered all his courage, and determined there and then that he would see it through to the end, whatever that end might be. I have looked death in the face before, and without flinching too, he thought. I can do it again. I must, or

never again call myself a knight. So keeping that thought firmly in mind now, Gawain got himself up and dressed and ready.

Outside his window the snow had fallen all around, silencing all but the crowing cockerel, and even his coarse cry was dulled and deadened by the snow. Servants brought him his mail coat first, cleaned now of any rust, and his body armour, as bright and shining again as it had been when he'd first set out from Camelot. Then he put on once more his scarlet surcoat, fur-lined to protect him against the cold – and of course he did not forget the green silk belt the lady had given him. This he wound securely around his waist, also for protection – not from the cold, but from death itself. He looked fine in it too, the gold thread of the belt glittering in the early sun that now streamed in through the window. It suits me well, this belt, thought Gawain, but I shouldn't care about what it looks like. It's the magic in this belt that I need, not its beauty.

When Gawain came downstairs, the guide was waiting as promised and Gringolet already saddled for him in the courtyard. The horse had been well fed and rested in his stable all this time, so his coat shone with health. He was fit and fiery again, fretting feverishly at his bit and tossing high his handsome head. Gawain could see his horse was itching to be off. Once Gawain was mounted he was handed his helmet and his shield, his sword and his spear. Gringolet was pawing the ground still, but Gawain held him back for a moment. "God keep all who live in this place," he said, looking up at the castle. "May he bless you for all your many kindnesses shown to me, a stranger. Lord and lady both, I wish you happiness and good fortune on this earth, and afterwards the place in heaven you both so richly deserve."

Now, as the drawbridge rattled down, he let Gringolet go at last. No spurs were needed, no squeeze of the legs: Gringolet leapt forward, sparks flying from his hooves, and galloped away over the drawbridge and out onto the snowy plain. Watching him go, the porter at the gate crossed himself three times and commended Gawain to God, for like everyone in the castle he knew what lay ahead of the knight that day and feared for his life.

Catching him up after a while, the guide led Gawain on more slowly now, through the mantle of freshly fallen snow. Soon their way took them up into inhospitable hills where an icy wind chilled their faces, then higher yet onto craggy moorland where mists hung dark about them. They trudged through stinking bogs, they waded through roaring rivers, until at last they found themselves passing under high overhanging cliffs and into deep dark woods where the wind whistled wildly through the branches above them.

When at last they rode out of this dreary place and into the sunlight, Gawain saw that he was on the crown of a hill, below which a sparkling stream flowed gently by. Here the guide, who until now had not spoken a word, reined in his horse and turned to speak to Gawain. "This is the place, Sir Gawain," he said, and his voice trembled with fear as he spoke. "Follow that stream and it will lead you to the Green Chapel and the fearsome knight who guards it. No bird sings there. No snow ever falls. No flowers bloom." Gawain thanked him, and made to ride on, but the guide grasped at his reins and held him back. "If you'll take my advice, Sir Gawain – and I know it is not my place to give it – you should not go any further. I have too much respect and love for you to let you go on without warning you. The man who awaits you is the most terrible knight alive, a real butcher, I promise you. He is not just the strongest knight that ever lived, but the most savage, the most vicious. He loves to kill, and is very good at it too, believe me. No man who has visited the Green Knight of the Green Chapel has ever lived to tell the tale. It's always the same. We find their bodies downstream, hacked and hewn to pieces. He shows no mercy to anyone, Sir Gawain. Page boy or priest, they're all meat to him. He'll feed you to the fishes, sir, like all the others. So don't go, I beg you." And now he spoke low, in a confidential whisper. "Listen, Sir Gawain. Why not go home another way? No one'll ever know. I shall tell no one that you changed your mind and thought better of it. Your reputation is safe with me, sir."

"Thanks all the same," Gawain replied, "I know you have only my best interests at heart, and I am grateful to you for that, but I've come this far – too far to turn tail and run now. I'm sure you would keep my cowardice a secret, but I would know, and I would not be able to live with myself. I am a Knight of King Arthur's court, and I have to keep the promise I made, even if I do end up as food for the fish. My courage is fragile enough as it is, so please don't try to talk me out of it any more."

"I have done all I can to save you," said the guide, sighing sorrowfully. "If you insist on going to your certain death, Sir Gawain, then I cannot stop you. To find the Green Knight, just ride along the stream until you see the Green Chapel on your left. Cross the stream and call out for him. He'll come. And then, God help you. No one else can. I shall leave you here, sir. For all the gold in the world I would not go where you are going. Goodbye, Sir Gawain." And touching his heels to his horse he rode away and left Gawain alone. Talk is easy enough, Gawain thought, but now I must be as good as my word and try to be the kind of knight I claim to be and others believe me to be.

So with a heavy heart he urged Gringolet down the hill towards the stream and, as his guide had told him, followed it, looking always for the first glimpse of the Green Chapel on the opposite bank. Still he saw nothing, but rode on through a deep ravine with jagged black rocks on either side that reared above him, shutting out the sun almost entirely. This is like the gateway to hell itself, thought Gawain.

As he came out of this dark ravine at last the valley widened around him, sunlight falling on a grassy mound beyond the stream, which here ran fast and furious. But still he saw no chapel, green or otherwise. Not a bird sang. There were no flowers, and no snow either. The path looked treacherous ahead of him, so Gawain thought that here might be the best place to cross – for although the stream rushed and roared, he could see the pebbles beneath and so knew it could not be too deep. He spurred Gringolet through the stream and up onto the bank beyond. As he came closer and rode around it, he could see that the grassy mound looked like some kind of burial barrow, with dark gaping entrances on all sides, a place of death.

Gawain dismounted by a wide oak tree, and leaving Gringolet to rest and graze he decided to explore further on foot. This neither looks nor feels like any chapel I've seen before, he thought. It seems to me more like the Devil's lair than God's holy chapel. Yet it is green, and it is certainly sinister enough to suit the Green Knight.

Grasping his spear firmly Gawain walked slowly around the barrow, searching for the Green Knight. He climbed right to the top so that he could see far and wide on all sides. Still he saw no one. But as he stood there he began to hear from the far side of the stream the sound of grinding, like an axe being sharpened on a stone. Gawain knew at once it was the Green Knight. He fingered his green silk belt nervously, making sure it was tight around him, and as he did so a sudden fierce anger welled up in him and drove away his fear. "If the

Green Knight thinks he can frighten me away," Gawain said to himself, "then he had better think again. I may die today, but I'll not die frightened. I won't give him the satisfaction."

He summoned up all his courage and called out loud, so loud that his voice could be heard over that incessant horrible rasping. "Gawain is here!" he cried. "Come out and show yourself. I am here as I promised I would be. But I won't wait for ever. Come out and do your worst."

"I won't be long," came the booming voice that Gawain recognized only too well. "I think my axe needs to be a little bit sharper still – just in case you have a tough neck on you." And the dreaded man, still hidden from Gawain's sight somewhere in amongst the rocks beyond the stream, laughed till the hills echoed with it. But some moments later, the last of the grim grinding done, the Green Knight stepped out from a cleft in the rocks, fingering the blade of his axe and smiling a cruel smile.

He was just as Gawain remembered, except that, incredibly, miraculously, his head was on his shoulders again. His hair and beard, green as before. His face and hands, green. And everything he wore was bright green too. He used his axe to vault the stream effortlessly, so crossed without even getting his feet wet, and then with huge strides came up the hill towards Gawain, growing bigger and broader, it seemed, with every step, until this mountain of a man stood before him, his blood-red eyes burning into his. Gawain had forgotten how terrifying those eyes were, but even so he managed to return the

Green Knight's gaze without wavering for a moment.

"You're most welcome, Sir Gawain, to my chapel," said the Green Knight, bowing low. "You've done well so far, very well. I said a year and a day from when we last met, and here you are. I said you would find me here at the Green Chapel, and you have. But that was the easy part. From now on you'll find it a little more difficult, I think. Last time we met, if you remember, I said you could deal me any blow you liked. You  showed me no mercy, but struck my head from my shoulders. Now, as we both agreed and promised then, it is my turn. So get yourself ready. And don't expect any mercy from me, either. I will give as good as I got from you."

"That was the bargain we made," Gawain replied, hiding as best he could the fear in his voice. "You don't hear me complaining, do you?" So he laid aside his helmet and spear and shield. "I'm ready when you are," he said. And clasping tight the silken belt to still his rising terror

– for he knew its magic was all that stood now between him and certain death – Gawain went down on one knee before the Green Knight and gritted his teeth to await the blow.

Round and round and round whirled the axe just above Gawain's head, so that the terrible breath of it parted his hair as it passed by. "Bare your neck, Sir Gawain," laughed the Green Knight. "I wouldn't want to hurt a hair on your head."

Gawain gathered his hair and bent his neck. "Get on with it, why don't you?" he cried.

"With pleasure," said the Green Knight. As the axe came down, slicing through the air, Gawain caught sight of it out of the corner of his eye, and shrank from the blow. But the blow never came. At the very last moment the Green Knight held back the blade, so that it touched neither the skin nor a single hair on his neck.

"What's the matter?" the Green Knight mocked. "The great Gawain is not frightened, is he? I haven't even touched you, and yet you flinch like a coward. Did I flinch when you made to strike me a year ago? No, I did not. Yet you kneel there shaking like a leaf. Shame on you, Gawain. I had thought better of a Knight of the Round Table."

Fuming now at these insults, and at his own weakness too, Gawain bent his head once more. "No more of your talk. This time I won't flinch, you have my word on it."

"We'll see," laughed the Green Knight. "We'll see." And once again he heaved up his axe high above his head. This time as the blade whistled down Gawain did not move a muscle, he did not even twitch. But once more the Green Knight held back the blade at the very last moment. "Just practising, Sir Gawain," said the Green Knight, smiling down at him. "Just practising."

Now Gawain was blazing with anger. "Next time you'd better do it!" he cried. "It will be your last chance, I promise you. On my knighthood I promise you that."

"Nothing can save you this time, Sir Gawain," said the Green Knight, wielding his axe. "Not even your precious knighthood will save your neck now."

"Do your worst," Gawain told him, resigned now to his fate. He closed his eyes and waited.

"As you wish," said the Green Knight. "Here it comes, then." He stood, legs apart, readying himself. Gripping his hideous axe he lifted it high and brought it down with terrible force onto the nape of Gawain's neck. This time the blade cut through the skin and the flesh beneath, but only a little, just enough to draw blood. No more. No deeper damage was done.

At the first sharp stab of pain and at the sight of his own blood on the ground Gawain leapt at once to his feet and drew his sword. "One chance is all you get," he cried. "I have kept my side of the bargain we made. If you come at me again, I shall defend myself to the death. Mighty though you are, you will feel the full fury of Gawain's sword."

Leaning now on his great axe the Green Knight looked at Gawain and smiled down on him in open admiration. "Small you might be, Gawain," he said, "but you have the heart and spirit of a lion. Put down your sword. We two have nothing to fight about. All I did, like you, was to keep the deal we made a year and a day ago. A blow for a blow, that was the pact between us. So let us consider the matter settled, shall we – all our debts to one another fully paid."

Lowering his sword, Gawain put his hand to his neck and felt how small a cut it was. "I don't understand," he said, as bewildered now as he was relieved. "You could easily have cut off my head with one blow. Yet you took three, and then you just nicked me. I lopped yours off at one stroke back at King Arthur's court. I showed you no mercy. Yet you spared my life. Why?"

The Green Knight stepped forward and offered Gawain his scarf to staunch his bleeding. "Think yourself back, Sir Gawain," he began, "to the castle you have just left. Think yourself back to the Christmas game you played with the lord of that castle."

"But how do you know about that?" Gawain asked.

"All in good time, Sir Gawain," laughed the Green Knight. "All in good time. Three times you and he promised to exchange whatever it was you managed to come by. The first time you were as good as your word, as was the lord of the castle – a kiss in exchange for a deer, I believe it was. Am I right?" Gawain could only nod – he was too astonished to speak. "So that was why just now I teased you the first time with my axe, and did not even touch you. Then, the second day at the castle, you again did just what you had promised. What was it? Two kisses for a giant boar – and what a boar that was too! Not a great bargain for the lord of the castle, but an honest one, and that's all that counts. Your neck is bleeding, my friend, because of what happened back at the castle on the third day. On that day when the lord returned from his hunt and presented you with that cunning old fox, all you gave him in return, I seem to recall, were the three kisses you received from his beautiful wife. But you forgot to hand over to me the green silken belt she gave you, the enchanted belt that could save your life, the one you're wearing now around your waist."

Gawain gaped aghast at the Green Knight, understanding at that moment that somehow this Green Knight and the lord of the castle must be one and the same. Gawain flushed to the roots of his hair, knowing his deceit and cowardice were now exposed. The Green Knight spoke kindly, though. "Yes, Gawain, my friend, I'm afraid I am both the men you think I am. How that can be I shall explain later. It was I who wanted to play our little game. It was I who sent my wife to your room to tempt you, to test your honour and chivalry to the limit – and she did, did she not? In everything except the silken belt you were as true and honourable as any knight that ever lived. Only the belt caught you out, for you hid it from me and did not hand it over as you should have done. You broke your word. For that one failure I nicked your neck and drew blood when I struck for the third time."

Gawain hung his head in shame now, unable to look the Green Knight in the eye. "Don't judge yourself too harshly, my friend," the Green Knight went on. "Three times you passed the temptation test and did not succumb to my wife's charms, and that took some doing. You hid the secret of the green silken belt only to save your own life. It is no great shame to want to live, my friend."

But Gawain tore off the silken belt and threw it to the ground. "How can I ever call myself a knight again after this?" he cried. "You and I both know the truth. I behaved like a coward, that's all there is to it. Say what you like, but I have failed myself and betrayed the most sacred vows of my knighthood."

Then the Green Knight laid his hand gently on Gawain's shoulder to comfort him. "No man is perfect, dear friend," he said. "But you are as near to it as I have ever met. You've paid your price – your neck's still bleeding, isn't it? And you've acknowledged your fault openly and honestly. Don't be so hard on yourself. All we can do is learn from our mistakes, and that I know you'll do." He bent down then and picked up the silken belt.

"Take it, Gawain," he said. "May it remind you whenever you wear it of what has happened here and back at my castle – both the pleasures

and the pain." Refusing to take no for an answer he tied the belt around Gawain's waist and stood back when it was done. "It suits you," he laughed. "And my wife was right, too. You are a handsome devil if ever I saw one. Now, Gawain, my dear friend, come back home with me and we can feast again together, and sit before the fire as we did before and talk long into the night. And don't worry, this time my wife will behave herself, I can guarantee it."

Tempted as he was by the warmth of the invitation, Gawain shook his head. "I cannot," he said. "You know how much I should like to stay, but I must be on my way. If I come back with you I might never want to leave. No, I must go back to King Arthur, to Camelot, as quickly as I can. I'm sure they'll be thinking the worst has happened to me." He set his helmet on his head and made ready to leave, the Green Knight helping him into the saddle. "And thank you for the gift of this belt," said Gawain, as the two friends clasped hands for the last time. "It will always remind me of you and your lady, of all that has happened to me here, of the wonderful days I have spent with you this Christmas time. But it will also serve to remind me of my failures and my frailties. It will prevent me from ever coming to believe in my own myth. It will help me to know myself for what I am."

"Go, then," said the Green Knight sorrowfully. "Go, and may God speed you home. We shall miss you and long for your return."

But settled now in his saddle Gawain did not want to leave without a few answers. "There is still much that I'm puzzled about," he said. "Who exactly are you? Which of you is you – if you know what I mean? Which is the real you? And who was the ancient craggy crone back at the castle who always watched me like a hawk? And tell me, how and why has all this happened to me?"

"After all you've been through you have a right to know everything," replied the Green Knight. "I am known in these parts as Bertilak of the High Desert. And the old lady you spoke of is Morgana le Fey, who learned her powerful magic from Merlin and uses it often to test the virtue of the Knights of the Round Table, and to corrupt them if she can. She is jealous of Arthur – she always has been. It was she who enchanted me, made me into the green giant you see before you, and sent me to Camelot a year and a day ago to discover whether the Knights of the Round Table are really as brave and chivalrous as they claim to be. How else, unless I was enchanted, could I have ridden off headless, and later grown my head again? How else could I be the green giant? And what's more, Gawain – and this will surprise you even more perhaps – that old woman is your aunt, King Arthur's own half-sister. I sometimes think there's nothing she likes more than causing King Arthur all the mayhem and mischief she can, and she can cause plenty. Still, so far, my friend, we've both survived all her machinations and her enchantments, haven't we? I will lose my greenness between here and my castle, and you will survive to go home. All has ended well."

There on that green barrow the two knights parted and went their separate ways, the one riding to his castle near by, the other setting out on the long journey back home to Camelot. It *was* long, too, and Gawain and Gringolet had a hard time of it. Hospitable houses were few and far between, so Gawain could never be sure of a warm bed and frequently found himself sleeping out in the open. The snow was often deep, and the paths precipitous and treacherous. But at least Gawain could be sure of the direction he was going, for the geese that had pointed his way to the lord's castle before Christmas flew over him once again like an arrow, a singing arrowhead in the sky, this time showing him his way back to Camelot, back home. As for Gringolet, he stepped out strongly all the way, as any horse does when he knows he's going home.

❖ ❖ ❖ SOME DAYS LATER THEY RODE AT LAST OVER THE DRAWBRIDGE INTO CAMELOT ❖ Everyone came rushing out to meet them, including the High King himself and Guinevere, his queen. Many tears were shed at Gawain's happy and unexpected homecoming, for although everyone had hoped and prayed for it, there was no one who had ever really expected to see him again – not in this life, anyway.

Sat by the fire in the great hall at Camelot, with everyone gathered around and a goblet of mulled wine warm in his hand, Gawain told his amazing story – they wouldn't let him eat a mouthful until he had. And to his credit he left nothing out, even those shameful parts of the story a lesser man would have kept hidden for ever. As proof of the truth of all he had told them, and of his shame, he bared his neck and showed them his scar. "And look, my lord King," said Gawain, undoing the green belt from around his waist. "Here is the belt I spoke of. Here is my badge of shame."

Later that evening, after the king and queen, all the knights and their ladies had feasted together to celebrate Gawain's safe return, King Arthur rose to his feet and toasted Gawain as a paragon of knightly virtues. He praised his nephew's honesty and integrity, his

chivalry and his courage. "He is a shining example for all of us
to follow," said the High King. "I have decided, therefore, in honour
of Sir Gawain, and to remind us always of our knightly vows and
virtues, that from now on, as a token of honour and purity,
we should wear a green silken belt embroidered
with gold, just like Gawain's."

AND TO THIS DAY,
HUNDREDS
OF YEARS LATER,

the greatest and worthiest knights in our land wear about them a silken belt much the same as was worn by the great Sir Gawain in his battle with the Green Knight. So his name lives on, my friends, as I hope his story will for many long years to come.